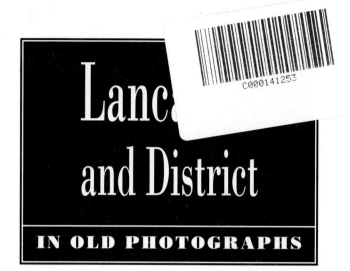

Lanca
and District

IN OLD PHOTOGRAPHS

Lancaster
and District

IN OLD PHOTOGRAPHS

Compiled by SUSAN ASHWORTH
and NIGEL DALZIEL

Alan Sutton Publishing Limited
Phoenix Mill · Far Thrupp
Stroud · Gloucestershire

ALAN SUTTON

First published 1993

Front cover illustration: The Duke and Duchess
of York (the future King George V) at Lancaster
Town Hall, Market Square, 1896. During their
visit to the town they opened the new Royal
Lancaster Infirmary and were presented with a
photograph album of local views taken by John
Davis & Sons.

Half title page: Sunderland Point fishermen
with their children, photographed by John
Walker, *c*. 1900.

Title page: Lower Church Street, looking
towards Stonewell, Lancaster, *c*. 1905. The
buildings on the right are now the site of the St
Nicholas Arcade shopping centre.

British Library Cataloguing in Publication Data

Ashworth, Susan
  Around Lancaster in Old Photographs
  I. Title II. Dalziel, Nigel
  942.769

ISBN 0-7509-0131-4

Typeset in 9/10 Sabon.
Typesetting and origination by
Alan Sutton Publishing Limited.
Printed in Great Britain by
Redwood Books, Trowbridge, Wiltshire.

Morecambe and Heysham athletic display team, 1930s.

Contents

Acknowledgements

The photographs in this volume have come mainly from the collections of Lancaster City Museums. We are grateful both to donors of original photographs and to the many others who allow us to copy their photographs to add to our collections. We would also like to thank the following people and organizations for providing information or for giving permission to use their photographs.

Dennis Aldren • Harry Allan • Sam Baxter • Roger Bingham • British Rail
Mr Briggs • Dr Carne • John Clarkson • Hugh Cunliffe • the *Daily Express*
The Dukes Theatre • Stuart Eastwood • Mrs Entwistle • Mrs Farrell
Forbo Kingfisher • Rose and Robert Gardner • Mr and Mrs Gerrard
Philip Gilchrist • Albert Gilham • Bill Houston • Maude Huck • The King's
Own Regimental Museum at Lancaster City Museum • the *Lancaster
Guardian* • Lancaster Reference Library • John MacKenzie • Morecambe
Reference Library • Mrs Mort • George Niven • David Alan Pennant
John Pryce • Sister Ada Rowe • The Royal Commission on the Historical
Monuments of England Crown Copyright • Mr Shackleton • Solo Agency
the Speight family • Gordon Sutcliffe • the *Visitor* newspaper
Michael Walker • Lynn Wilman • Dr Michael Winstanley.

The authors would also like to thank the staff of Lancaster City Museums for their support and assistance in producing this volume – whether in terms of advice and information or in fielding enquiries to allow time to be spent at the word processor.

Golden Ball Yard, Lancaster, photographed by Sam Thompson, 9 May 1926.

Introduction

In the age before the camera, artists of both local and national repute painted the stylish town of Lancaster and its picturesque surroundings. Not least among these were J.M.W. Turner and David Cox. However, it is the arrival of the camera and its use to record the changing landscapes and communities in the area that concern us here.

Although pioneering work in photography was taking place in the 1840s, the Lancaster region does not appear to have been captured by the medium for another twenty years. Even then photography was such an expensive and painstaking process that few people were able to pursue it. The City Museums hold only a handful of images from the 1860s (pp. 7 and 22).

Revd Chippendall and his niece at St Patrick's chapel ruins, Heysham, 1861. This is probably the earliest photograph in the museums' collections and was taken by local amateur photographer J. Lawson Whalley.

Carte de visite portrait of an unknown young woman photographed by J.N. Stockdale of Damside Street, Lancaster around 1878. Stockdale is listed in local directories between 1881 and 1896.

Back of a Pandolfini & Fawcett carte de visite, *c.* 1880, suggesting a close link between the work of photographers and artists. A tiny view of Lancaster, with a figure rowing on the River Lune, is just visible to the right.

The earliest mention of 'professional photographers' in Lancaster is in the 1850s. In 1851 W. Bannister could take your likeness, in his caravan by the King Street Assembly Rooms, for anything from 5s to 16s 6d. Messrs Partington & Paterson announced they would be taking portraits in Mrs Cass's garden, behind Market Street, for two weeks in the spring of 1854.

As photographic techniques developed a number of professionals established studios in the town. The earliest entries in directories are from 1864, when there were three firms in Lancaster and three in Morecambe.

These studios were particularly popular for their portraits. Many examples of card-mounted portraits in the standard small (carte de visite) and larger (cabinet card) sizes can be found stamped and decorated with the names of local photographic businesses (p. 8). They were much cheaper than earlier portraits – at 5s for a dozen carte de visites in 1896 – and so were within reach of many more families.

Some firms traded for several generations (Davis & Sons, 1869 to around

1935) and some seem to have been run by flamboyant local characters. In Signor Randolphe Pandolfini's obituary, for example, it was said that he was an Italian count with a diplomatic service record in France and Dublin before

John Walker (right) at the Watch House, Glasson Dock, c. 1900. Walker's father and grandfather were harbourmasters in Lancaster. Although trained as a solicitor, John does not seem to have worked for a living. He was a member of Lancaster Photographic Society from 1894 to 1902, when he was struck off the membership for subscription arrears.

John Walker's parlour – either in Aldcliffe Road, Lancaster, or at Sunderland Point. Walker, a bachelor, lived with his mother and two unmarried sisters. They had houses in both places. At some point the family 'fortunes' failed and Walker died, in 1939, in Lancaster Workhouse.

Sam Thompson's portrait of local artist John Crane (1850–1915) working at Marshaw Wyre, near the Trough of Bowland, around 1910. Thompson worked for a printing firm in Lancaster, Rembrandt Intaglio. In his spare time he recorded many of the local characters of the area. His portraits won awards in exhibitions during the 1930s, and some were also shown in America and Canada in a selection of 'the Best of British' compiled by the Royal Photographic Society.

St Mary's Place, Lancaster, photographed by Sam Thompson on 16 May 1927. On the 1892 town map there are forty-five titled yards, courts and alleys, and many more are unnamed. Many were cleared in the 1920s and 1930s. Mitre House, at the top of Church Street, now stands on the site of this court.

his arrival in Lancaster in the 1870s. In the 1890s Pandolfini also taught Italian and French at the local Storey Institute.

Local buildings and landscape views by professional photographers are found in many books and guides to the area as well as in postcard format (p. 19). For a more detailed historical view of the district, however, we owe a great deal to the enthusiastic and skilful local amateurs.

Main Street, Hornby, *c.* 1920. On the right is the Hornby Institute, built in 1906 by the Foster family of Hornby Castle and leased to the village trust at a peppercorn rent. The bridge over the Wenning was widened during the Second World War to allow bigger vehicles to travel up the valley.

Holiday crowds on Morecambe front, *c.* 1906. In the background is the town's Central Pier, first opened in 1869. The clock tower was the gift of Alderman J.R. Birkett in 1905.

Iris Waller, Miss Great Britain 1956, in Morecambe's Super Swimming Stadium with one of the competition judges, Charles Eade. The competition originated in the resort in 1945.

The Taming of the Shrew in Williamson Park, summer 1992. With the Ashton Memorial as a dramatic backdrop to the scene, the Dukes Theatre, Lancaster, provides another in its excellent series of promenade theatre productions. Photograph by Arthur Thompson.

The individual photographers known to us had particular interests in recording the changing streets, local communities and well-known individuals of the area. The City Museums' collections would be much the poorer, for example, without John Walker's Sunderland Point and fishing community photographs (p. 1) or Sam Thompson's systematic recording of streets, yards and alleys scheduled for demolition (pp. 6 and 11), not to mention his interest in the faces of local 'characters' (pp. 10 and 43). Many of Lancaster's streets were captured by Albert Gilham's camera in the 1960s, another period of great change in the city (p. 27). The list could carry on and on.

Lancaster City Museums try to represent the whole of our district within the photographic collections. However, our undoubted strengths are in the Lancaster and Morecambe areas – as this volume testifies.

We are still collecting historic photographs wherever possible and are copying others lent by local owners. We are also attempting to carry on some of the work of Sam Thompson and Albert Gilham in recording changes to the landscape, current events (p. 13) and so on. The City Museum Service would be glad to hear from anyone who can help us with this work.

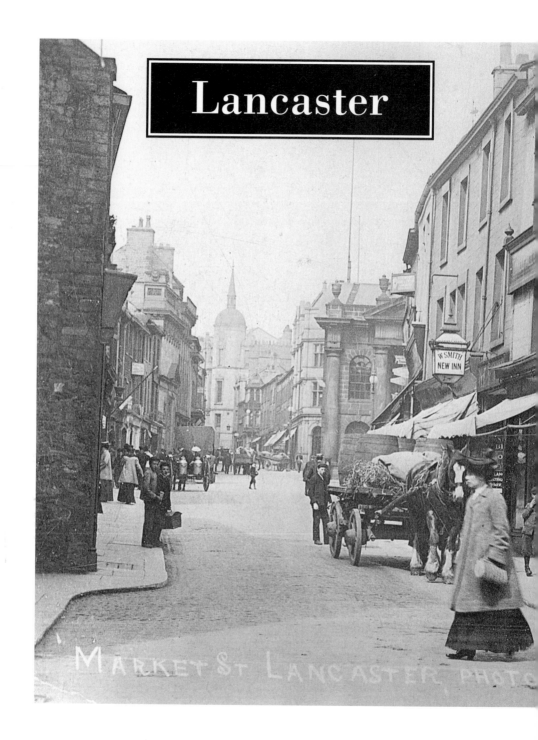

Lancaster

W SMITH
NEW INN

MARKET ST LANCASTER, PHOTO

John o'Gaunt's gateway to Lancaster Castle, photographed by Sam Thompson on 17 May 1927. The natural rise in the land, standing at the lowest crossing point of the River Lune, provided an excellent defensive site. It was used as such from Roman times onwards. The gateway is thought to date from around 1400. The statue of John o'Gaunt, the second Duke of Lancaster, was set in place in 1822 and was carved by Claude Ninno. To the left is a British First World War tank next to the oak tree which was planted by Queen Victoria during her visit to Lancaster in 1851. The iron railings were dismantled for munitions during the Second World War.

Previous page: Market Street from Horseshoe Corner, *c.* 1905.

Ceremonial arrival of Herbert Lushington Storey, high sheriff of Lancashire, at the Shire Hall in 1904. The new high sheriff placed a coat of arms in the Hall each year. This part of the castle, with new court rooms, was built in the early 1800s. Lancaster had been the location for court hearings, or assizes, twice a year from 1166 until 1972 – when Preston Crown Court was opened. It was the only Lancashire town with such court sessions until 1835, when Liverpool's courts opened.

After a confirmation service at St Mary's parish church, 1906. Standing next to the castle, St Mary's has been the parish church since 1430, but for many it is still known as the priory. In 1094 Roger de Poitou, the local landowner, gave the priory to the Abbey of Sees in Normandy. Benedictine monks were installed. Much of the building dates from the 1400s, although the tower (1755), Kings Own Chapel (1903) and porch are later additions.

'The Great Freeze' – ice on the River Lune at Ford Quay, photographed by Sam Thompson on 12 February 1895. Lancaster's wealth was based on its trading links with the West Indies in the 1700s. At one point it was the fourth largest port in England trading with the West Indies. In the background is Lune Mills, Lancaster's vast linoleum factory belonging to James Williamson & Sons, the town's major employer in Victorian times.

The old Town Hall, Market Square, decorated for the coronation of Edward VII and photographed by John Walker in 1902. The Town Hall, now housing the City Museum, was opened in 1783. To the right (with the telegraph poles) was the central office of the National Telephone Company, established in Lancaster in 1885. Next door were the police and fire stations housed in the former Commercial Hotel – now the site of the library.

Dalton Square in a Davis & Sons postcard, *c.* 1905. This was the eastern boundary of medieval Lancaster. It was the site of another monastery, the Friary. The Wesleyan church (centre) is thought to stand over its buildings. The land became the property of the Dalton family of Thurnham Hall and was sold off for development in 1784. The porched building, Palatine Hall, was Lancaster's first Catholic chapel (1798). It later became an entertainments hall, a cinema and is now part of the City Council offices. Next door is the house and surgery that became infamous in 1935 when Dr Buck Ruxton murdered his wife, Isabel, and their maidservant Mary Rogerson.

Unloading coal at White Cross Mill, *c.* 1950. Lancaster Canal opened in 1797 and caused great changes to the town's industry. Heavy goods, particularly coal to fire the steam engines, could now be delivered in bulk to canal-side mills, the first of which opened at White Cross in 1802. The new cotton mills soon attracted many new workers into town.

Winder's Court off Monmouth Street, photographed by Sam Thompson on 20 May 1927. Many of the courts and yards date from the early 1800s, when there was a heavy demand for housing for workers in the new cotton-spinning mills of the town. Most were built by infilling town-centre space. Like this one, most courts had a communal water supply. Note also the large mangle tucked under the entrance to the court.

Chancery Lane, looking from the Market Square end towards Church Street, *c.* 1905. There are no longer any houses in this lane although it still provides a short cut to the town centre.

A street party in Dyehouse Lane for the coronation of George VI in 1937. This particular street disappeared under the new bus station which opened in 1939. In 1846 the lane was noted as having some of the poorest-quality housing, and the cheapest rents in the town at 1s 6d a week.

Penny Street canal bridge, the southern entrance to Lancaster, *c.* 1865. This was one of the sites for toll collections from traders bringing their goods into market. The others were on Skerton Bridge and St Leonardgate. In 1887 James Williamson, the local linoleum magnate, bought out the tolls (for £1,500) to ensure market goods could be sold more cheaply.

Church Street on market day, looking towards the Judges' Lodgings, *c.* 1900.

Men of the 1st Royal Lancashire Militia outside Springfield Barracks, South Road, *c.* 1860. The building was completed in 1855 and has had many uses: it housed the Militia until 1881, when they moved to Bowerham Barracks (now St Martin's College); it was the property of Storey Bros. coated fabrics for almost a century and now holds small, service-industry units, including Granada TV.

Engineer Lancaster with some of its men, *c.* 1905. The engine was built in 1857 as a goods engine. It was adapted to passenger transport and renamed in 1895. The engine was cut up in 1911. The railways arrived in Lancaster, from Preston, in 1840. In 1846 the line was extended to Carlisle. This new and faster means of transport put immediate pressure on the canal company and its services.

Laying tram tracks in South Road, *c*. 1902. To supply the electricity for the tram service the Corporation had to build a new power station in Marton Street. The service's twelve trams were built in Lancaster at the local Wagon Works on Caton Road.

The first tram of the service, driven by Alderman Jackson, in Dalton Square on 14 January 1903. The first depot was on the site of the current Town Hall in Dalton Square. With the new civic buildings it was moved to the top of Thurnham Street, where part of it survives today as a garage.

Brock Street, *c.* 1908. Boots the Chemist (left) first came to Lancaster in 1899. The open-top trams had roofs fitted in 1911 and a number were cut down into single-deckers in 1920. Although the trams were well used, the town was not large enough to sustain the service. The trams stopped running in 1930 when the last one was driven – like the first – by Alderman Jackson.

Beer delivery by horse and dray to the Park Hotel, Bowerham Road, *c.* 1900. The horse remained the primary means of moving goods around the area, although many of the shops employed errand boys to deliver smaller amounts on foot, by handcart or later by bicycle.

Postcard view of King Street by Davis & Sons, *c.* 1905. The carriage is turning into Common Garden Street with its fascia indicating the Market Hall. The shop behind the policeman was James Wilson's grocers. It is said that the shop floor fell through during a closing auction of contents. It was full of people at the time.

The demolition and redevelopment of the market site, photographed by Albert Gilham in 1960, from Common Garden Street looking towards King Street. Penny's Almshouses (left) and the King's Arms (right) are visible in the background. This same area is undergoing further redevelopment in the near future.

The courtyard of Penny's Almshouses, *c.* 1900. Established by the will of William Penny in 1720, the almshouses were for twelve poor men. Women could be offered a house if there were insufficient needy men. They were modernized in 1974 and are run today by Lancaster Charities, which houses about sixty local people.

Postcard view of the Royal Lancaster Infirmary, by Davis & Sons, c. 1900. Health care for poorer folk was originally provided through the Dispensary, a charitable institution established by a Dr Campbell in 1781 and funded through subscriptions. In 1896 the Infirmary was opened by the Duke and Duchess of Gloucester, the future King George V and Queen Mary.

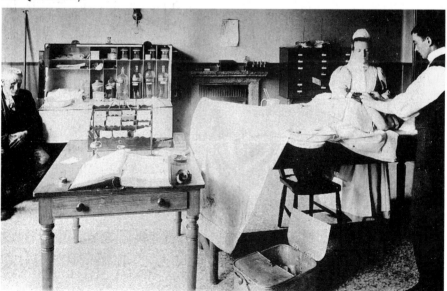

Casualty Room in the new Royal Lancaster Infirmary, c. 1897. With a number of large hospitals in the area nursing was one of several occupations for local women; others included weaving, domestic service and shop work.

Dalton Square in 1909 with its new layout including the Town Hall – the gift of Lord Ashton (James Williamson, the linoleum magnate). Lord Ashton was one of several local benefactors who changed the townscape. The building was designed by E.W. Mountford, architect of the Old Bailey, and incorporates furniture by Waring & Gillow and stained glass by the local firm of Shrigley & Hunt.

Group of art school staff at the Storey Institute, with the principal (Charles Ripper) seated in the middle, photographed by Davis & Sons, *c.* 1900. The Storey Institute was the gift of Thomas Storey (Williamson's main rival in coated fabrics). It opened as a technical school and art school, on the site of the earlier Mechanics Institute, in 1891.

Queen Victoria's statue in Dalton Square thronged with crowds on the occasion of Queen Elizabeth's visit to Lancaster on 13 April 1955. The statue was designed by Herbert Hampson for Lord Ashton. It was supposed to be set high in Williamson Park, but was relocated to Dalton Square after the Ashton Memorial was decided upon for the park.

Queen Elizabeth II with Prince Philip on the Town Hall steps in Dalton Square, accompanied by the mayor, Thomas Hully, on 13 April 1955. Since the time of King Henry IV (1399–1413) the monarch has been the Duke of Lancaster. Celebrations of royal events and royal visits have always been popular in the town.

The Corporation's electricity department float in Market Street during the 1897 procession to celebrate Queen Victoria's Diamond Jubilee.

Market Square from the portico of the City Museum (formerly the Town Hall), photographed by Mr Shackleton in 1937. Market Square, as its name suggests, has played host to the town's markets before they moved elsewhere. The square has thronged with folk during local celebrations, ox-roastings, processions and so forth. Here a quieter gathering is passing the time of day. Note the car in the background. The square was pedestrianized in the 1970s.

Waterfall, Williamson Park.

The cascade in Williamson Park on a decorative postcard, postmarked 1909. The park was a gift to the town from James Williamson & Sons, linoleum producers. The site had been open moorland, used as quarries for the town's great building period during the eighteenth century. The beginnings of a park had been laid out by unemployed labourers during the 'Cotton Famine' of the 1860s, when the American Civil War starved the cotton towns of Lancashire of raw materials. It was completed in 1881.

The Ashton Memorial, at the highest point of Williamson Park, *c.* 1920. Queen Victoria's statue (in Dalton Square) was originally meant to stand here. While improvements were being made to the park Lord Ashton's (James Williamson's) second wife, Jessie, died and this building was erected as a monument to her. It has been restored recently and forms the centre-piece of many of the Dukes Theatre promenade productions that take place in the park during the summer.

Boating for pleasure on Lancaster Canal, photographed by John Walker, *c.* 1900. From its outset in 1797 the canal was used for scheduled transport (packet-boats), industrial transport (barges) and for pleasure cruising – as it still is today.

Lancaster Cycling Club, photographed by J. Stockdale outside the castle in 1894. This was a time of growing popularity for the sport. The club saw its membership rise from 58 to 158 in 1893, with increasingly more women joining. Bicycles could be expensive. At about £15 the new improved Safety Cycles – which were taking over from the Ordinarys (or penny farthings as we know them) – were roughly equivalent to a year's salary for a young servant or a junior nurse.

The circus arrives in town, photographed by John Walker in Market Street, c. 1890. This was probably George Sanger's Hippodrome, Circus and Menagerie, which visited the town twice every summer, and performed on Giant Axe Field. In 1893 it boasted 295 men, women and children from all nations, 320 horses and ponies and 12 carriages of wild animals.

Lancaster Water Polo Team at the baths in 1894. The pool, along with public baths and a wash-house, had been opened in 1863 as a gift of the local MP Samuel Gregson. It stood on Cable Street, the site of Sainsbury's supermarket. In 1893 a new, larger pool was added where galas, races and water-polo matches were held. Kingsway pool was opened on 1 July 1939 replacing the old baths.

Lancaster Harriers, prizewinners in an unknown event, c. 1925. Sports have always been popular in the area, with local football, rugby, rowing, archery and bowling clubs – as well as the cycling, swimming and running groups seen here. Note the state of the runners' footwear compared to the trainers of today.

Evacuees from Salford gathered at Greaves School on 1 September 1939. Six trains, full of children and their teachers from Salford and Liverpool, arrived at Lancaster on this day. A total of almost 3,000 children arrived here during September. By Christmas only 800 were still here to join the parties laid on for them.

Staff of the Auxiliary Fire Service (AFS) photographed outside the fire station, behind the Town Hall in Dalton Square, *c.* 1940. By June 1939 some 130 volunteers had joined the local AFS to play their part in the civil defence arrangements for the town. Fortunately, this area was relatively clear of air-raid attacks.

Women's Voluntary Service (WVS) helping with the salvage collection of aluminium and non-ferrous metals at the collection point, Middle Street School, August 1940. The WVS had been enrolling women since 1938 to help with all kinds of organizational tasks: billeting evacuees, canteen services, washing parties, salvage collection and so on. By 1940 there were 1,659 women in the service.

The City
at Work

Three generations building a hayrick – probably around Sunderland Point or Overton – photographed by John Walker, *c*. 1900. With rich agricultural land in the area, farming has long been a major occupation.

Sheep shearing in Barbon using hand clippers, *c*. 1900. Mechanical sheep-shearing clippers were introduced from Australia in the 1890s, but it is doubtful whether these machines were much in use in the countryside before the First World War.

Previous page: marking out the field for ploughing, probably somewhere near Sunderland Point, photographed by John Walker, *c*. 1900.

Unnamed milkmaid photographed by Sam Thompson in the 1890s. She is holding the traditional three-legged stool which could balance, without tipping over, on the uneven ground of the farmyard. Her bonnet kept the sun off her neck while she worked. Although working in dirty conditions, Victorian ideas of propriety would not allow her to wear trousers or a shorter skirt. Sam Thompson's parents were farmers in Scotforth. He would have known most of the local farming families and recorded many of them in his portraits.

The village blacksmiths, Scotforth, photographed at work by Sam Thompson, *c.* 1927. The blacksmith's shop was an important centre of production in every town and village – making and mending tools, preparing shoes for horses and so on. In Scotforth it stood at the crossroads of the main road and Hala Road, on the site of Booths supermarket. James Reay (left) took over the business in the late 1920s or early 1930s and is still listed there in a town directory of 1956.

The staff of the Greta Bank Pottery, Stone Jar and Bottle Manufacturers, at work, *c.* 1900. A number of small family-run potteries worked around Burton in Lonsdale, making use of the local clay and coal. From the mid-1700s to 1945, when the last firm closed, there were about fifteen different potteries in business. Greta Pottery specialized in making vessels for wine and spirit merchants in North Lancashire, Cumbria and Yorkshire. It was established around 1850 by James Parker, but was taken over by William Bateson in 1887 and remained in the family until it closed in 1938.

Gillow's machine-shop staff at the North Road workshops, Lancaster, in 1887. With Lancaster's strong trading links in the West Indies in the 1700s, a young joiner – Robert Gillow – seized the opportunity of turning exotic, imported, woods into fine furniture. His cabinet-making firm was to become a hallmark of quality craftsmanship in the town. Gillow & Co. made furniture for the Houses of Parliament in 1849 and gained its Royal Appointment in 1863.

Mr Lever, a master cabinet-maker, working on a piece of furniture at the Waring & Gillow 'Homemaking Exhibition' held at their London showrooms on Oxford Street in 1925. The Gillow family had no more to do with the firm from the early 1800s. In 1903 Gillow merged with the Liverpool cabinet-makers, Waring. The Lancaster workshops closed down in 1962.

Storey Bros. float, with a cotton-weaving power loom, ready for the 1897 procession through Lancaster to celebrate Queen Victoria's Diamond Jubilee (p. 32). Cotton mills were built in Lancaster from the early 1800s. By the middle of the century they were being bought up by two local families, the Williamsons and the Storeys, to make their coated-fabric businesses self-sufficient. By 1860 the two companies were the town's major employers.

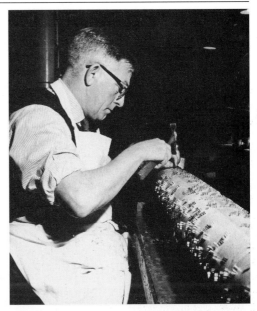

A roller cutter at work at Williamson & Sons, *c.* 1950. One of the many skilled jobs in the works was to produce rollers for the huge printing machines. As many as fifteen different colours, on individual rollers, could be used in a pattern and each one had to match up exactly. The designer's picture was broken down into a series of single colours and the pattern in that colour was produced from single pinheads or strips of brass set into a roller.

Women making inlaid linoleum at Williamson & Sons in the 1950s. This was the best quality lino. Instead of the pattern being printed on to the surface, which could wear away with usage, inlaid lino was made up of a jigsaw of coloured pieces of 'composition'. The pattern went right through to the backing fabric.

The 5th Battalion of the King's Own Regiment leaving their Lancaster billets (at the disused Wagon Works on Caton Road) for Didcot on 14 August 1914. The army – and particularly the local regiment – was one of Lancaster's many employers of local men, especially during the First World War. The 5th Battalion had just returned from a week in Barrow, guarding the docks.

Corporation electric buses in Market Square, *c.* 1916. Many women, both from the local area and further afield, found employment in various factories turning their production over to war work. These three buses are waiting to take the workforce down to the National Projectile shell-case factory on Caton Road.

Women at Waring & Gillow, cabinet-makers, sewing the fabric coverings of aircraft wings in 1917. The skills of furniture-makers were particularly useful with the growing demand for wooden-framed aircraft. Furniture manufacturers up and down the country were given over to such production.

Filling shells at the National Projectile factory on White Lund, *c*. 1916. This was the site of a major fire and devastating explosions on the night of Monday 1 October 1917. Shrapnel travelled miles in all directions; some examples survive today as souvenirs. Local people were evacuated to the surrounding countryside. Luckily the night shift was gathered in the works' canteen during their supper hour and were led to safety. By the Saturday ten bodies were recovered from the debris of the site. They were mainly firemen. The disaster was not reported in the press – for security reasons – just as the site did not appear on maps of the period. The cause of the fire was never found although some local people suspected foul play by enemy saboteurs.

Making tail sections at Williamson & Sons, oilcloth and linoleum manufacturers, *c.* 1945. During the Second World War women were conscripted for war work for the first time in history. This could be in munitions factories, in other factories given over to wartime production – such as here – or in one of the services, such as the Wrens or the Land Army. As coated-fabric producers, Williamsons were also useful producing such items as gas-proof clothing. Waring & Gillow made such things as tents, camouflage netting and forces' sleeping bags.

Shop fronts in St Nicholas Street, photographed by Sam Thompson on 18 April 1894. This was a busy shopping street and thoroughfare from Market Street to Stonewell, where the trams for Morecambe terminated. In 1893 plans were laid to widen the street. In May 1894 the shops on this side of the road were compulsorily purchased. Sam Thompson, acting in character, recorded the shops and their owners before the demolition began. The only objection to the scheme came from Mrs Parker, whose deceased husband had established the Boot and Shoe Warehouse on the right some thirty-seven years before. After long negotiations she was allowed to use the house and shop at the corner of Cheapside and St Nicholas Street while the Corporation demolished her premises and rebuilt it for her on the new building line.

Ullswater Road branch of the local Co-op, *c.* 1900. The Lancaster Co-op began trading in 1861 in an old flour warehouse on Penny Street. Its first branch in Galgate opened the same year. The Ullswater Road branch opened in September 1889. Note the young errand boy with the handcart for a home-delivery service. Although no longer a Co-op, the site is still a retail premises today.

Whittaker's cleaning service, *c.* 1905. Whittaker's house furnishers were established in Lancaster in 1863. They offered an all-round service, from removals and storage to furnishing and upholstery and – as this photograph shows – aftercare and cleaning. The business changed hands in 1992 and is now called The Furniture Shop.

William Hartley (left) and his staff outside his boot repair premises in Sir Simon's Arcade, Lancaster, *c.* 1905. Hartley is listed in local directories from 1901 to the 1950s.

Postcard of Pipers' Penny Bazaar and staff on Cheapside, Lancaster, taken by P. Turner, *c.* 1926. Just as Hartley's (above) had a young errand boy so Pipers have a young girl on their staff, who is learning the ropes.

An unnamed bargee on Lancaster Canal, photographed by Sam Thompson, *c.* 1927. Although much of the canal's trade had been taken over by the railways, some heavy goods – such as coal or slate – were still delivered by barge. Some bargees worked independently, on their own vessels, while others were employed by canal carriers. His 'bucket' was probably used for feeding his draught-horses. Sam Thompson was fascinated by the faces of characters and took many portraits of working men and women in the area.

Lancaster's Fire Brigade, with their new motor-driven engine, behind the new Town Hall in 1912. This engine replaced the horse-drawn steam engine they had acquired twenty years earlier. In 1910 the fire brigade moved to its new station buildings behind the Town Hall, on George Street. It was on the move again in August 1973 when it took up its present premises in Cable Street opposite Sainsbury's.

Lancaster Police, with Chief Constable Webb, grouped on one of the manual horse-drawn fire-engines in the corner of Market Square, *c.* 1890. The town's police force was in charge of the fire brigade until the latter was nationalized in 1941. Both services shared the buildings of the former Commercial Hotel, on the site of the library, using the stables for the horses and engines. In 1910 both were given new premises within the Town Hall complex in Dalton Square.

The first motor patrol vehicles of the Lancaster Borough Police: BSA 750 cc motor bikes and side-cars. PC Wilson is on the right. Lancaster's City Police force was amalgamated with Lancashire on 1 April 1947. They moved to the new building on Thurnham Street in October 1966.

Morecambe

Bare village, *c.* 1904. The name Morecambe was not adopted by the town until the last part of the nineteenth century. The area comprised the ancient villages of Bare, Poulton-le-Sands and Torrisholme. These were fishing and farming communities.

The Gerrard brothers unloading mussels near the Central Pier, *c.* 1900. This was the first pier in the town, opened in 1869. The elaborate pavilion was added in 1897 and was known in the area as the 'Taj Mahal'. The traditional trades survived alongside the new business of the town as a seaside resort.

Previous page: novelty postcard for Morecambe, postmarked 1908 and produced in London. This design, showing two young women with a life-belt, was used for a number of different resorts by substituting the name and an appropriate seaside scene.

The prom with the stone jetty of Morecambe harbour, *c*. 1890. Note the bathing machines, known locally as 'vans'. These were for changing in and, once pulled down into the sea by a horse, allowed the occupant to slip into the water unseen. In 1853 there were eighteen vans in the resort.

Morecambe sands with the West End Pier in the background, *c*. 1900. This pier was opened in 1896. Note the bathing machine in the water and the local traders making the most of the crowds of visitors. The resort began to grow after the coming of the railway in 1848. However, many of its grander attractions started appearing in the 1880s and 1890s.

Central Pier, *c.* 1936. The Central Pier was devastated by fire in 1933. Its replacement was opened in 1935, a stylish modern design in the latest fashion. Its twice-daily variety shows and ballroom dancing were popular pastimes for visitors.

Children's rides on Morecambe sands, in front of the Midland Hotel, *c.* 1950. The period between the two world wars was a time of expansion and growth in Morecambe. The Midland Hotel, built in 1933 to the designs of Oliver Hill, incorporated the latest ideas of art and design, including commissioned pieces by renowned modern artists of the day.

An enthralled audience, *c.* 1930. The Punch and Judy show goes back to Italian theatre of the 1500s and 1600s, known as the Commedia dell'Arte. Puppet masters made their own puppets and often added extra characters – and modern side stories – to the traditional storyline.

A 'blacked-up' minstrel group performing, in the old-fashioned way (alfresco), on the sands by West End Pier around 1935. Musical troupes were always popular in Morecambe. At first performances were only allowed on the sands, but by the early years of this century troupes were performing on the piers and in pavilions around the resort.

Hart's Pierrots troupe performing on Central Pier in 1906. In the 1890s came the new fashion for pierrot groups. They had distinctive costumes and whitened their faces with a mixture of zinc and lard. Women started to be included in performing troupes around the same time.

To launch the season: the Arcadian Follies variety troupe taking a ride on the Figure Eight dipper, c. 1938. The troupe was formed in 1934 by Ernest Binns, a local showman who had been with early groups such as 'The Wavelets' and 'The Merry Japs'. They performed in a pavilion alongside the fairground, where Frontierland now stands.

The Winter Gardens, *c.* 1935. This major entertainment hall was first opened in 1878 as the People's Palace of Varieties and Aquarium. In 1897 it almost doubled in size with the addition of the Victoria Pavilion – where there was a full variety show, twice daily. The Winter Gardens now boasted accommodation for about 4,000 people. Faced with such competition, the Summer Gardens – on the site of Regent Park – could not survive. It closed down around the turn of the century. The fate of the Winter Gardens – to demolish or refurbish? – is currently in the balance.

The Tower Ballroom, *c.* 1910. The Tower was opened, unfinished, in 1902. The central structure was to be an elaborate 'helter-skelter' type tower, leading to a viewing platform with splendid views across Morecambe Bay. It was removed, supposedly for munitions use, in the First World War. The site was renamed the Gaumont in 1949. It closed in 1959 and opened the next year as a ten-pin bowling alley. It is now a bingo hall.

The Alhambra Theatre, *c.* 1905. The hall opened in 1901 and ran a varied programme to suit all tastes: variety shows, films and dancing. Gradually it became clear that cinema was killing off live acts. In 1927 the Alhambra became a cinema and changed its name to the Astoria in 1930. The building was the main setting for the 1960 film *The Entertainer*, starring Laurence Olivier.

A busy dance floor in the Central Pier Ballroom, *c.* 1947. The pier was rebuilt in 1935 after a fire. Its previous ballroom, refurbished ten years earlier, included a decorative fountain in the centre. The dance craze was such that the crush on the floor occasionally resulted in dancers falling into the water. Central Pier boasted the last ballroom in the resort. It closed in November 1970. After five years of doubt the pier was finally demolished in 1992.

The Empire, *c.* 1940. Notice the women in military service uniform (centre and right). The complex was underway at the beginning of the Second World War. Despite government building restrictions this site was allowed to be completed. It incorporated a ballroom – the Floral Hall – and a cinema that could seat 1,500 people.

The front with the stone jetty and T.W. Wards shipbreakers in the background, *c.* 1908. Once Heysham harbour had opened in 1904 the stone jetty was no longer used for shipping services and was leased to the Sheffield-based company. Local worthies felt the shipbreaking did nothing for the status of the resort. Visitors to Morecambe thought otherwise. Wards became another of the local attractions.

Visitors to Wards shipbreakers on board the cruiser *Glasgow*, *c.* 1927. Once the ships were broken up, fixtures and furnishings were sold by auction. The yard proved itself a major attraction. Between 1921 and 1928 some 419,000 people paid to have a look at the ships in the yard, producing over £10,000 in entry fees. The yard closed in 1933 when the Corporation made a series of improvements to the proms.

The boating lake at Happy Mount Park, *c.* 1936. Visitors to Morecambe have always been fascinated by boats, whatever the size (p. 101). Happy Mount Park was opened in 1927.

Holidaymakers, on their return from a sailing trip around the bay, alighting by the Central Pier, *c.* 1948. Local fishermen took their boats out for regular pleasure cruises around the bay (p. 91).

Joint winners of the 1937 Cross Bay Swim, Dorothy Simpson and Kathleen Hodson, with a dead heat of four hours and fifty minutes. The challenge of the Cross Bay Swim began in 1907, when the local Victoria Bathing Club approached Professor Stearne of Manchester, a professional swimmer. His first effort at the ten-mile course was just beaten (by thirty-five seconds) by another Manchester man, Brierley Law of Chadderton, in the same year.

Postcard view of the inside of the new Super Swimming Stadium, postmarked 1938. The pool opened in 1936 in the harbour area of the resort. It was 110 yards long and was claimed to be the biggest outdoor pool in Europe, taking 1,250,000 gallons of water to fill. The pool could take 1,200 bathers and as many as 3,000 spectators – each paying, originally, a sixpence entrance fee. There was also a complex of steam, pine, foam and seaweed baths.

Commissionaire for the Super Swimming Stadium, 1958. During the season shows like water ballets or diving displays were held twice daily. The 'Miss Great Britain' beauty contest began here in 1945 (pp. 82 and 83).

Leaving the high diving board of the Super Swimming Stadium during the 1950s. Plans to roof over the pool in the 1960s came to nothing when it was clear that major overall repairs were needed. In 1975 the pool closed down. Four years later a smaller 'fun pool' opened on the site, followed in 1990 by 'Bubbles'.

Members of the Kinning Park Pipe Band, with three bathing beauties from the fashion parade of Windsor Water Woollies swimsuits, on Central Pier, 18 July 1933. The pipe band was performing as part of the year's Scottish Week events, when the resort provided themed entertainments for the many visitors from Glasgow and Aberdeen who were in town.

Opposite (top)
Performance at the Harbour Band Arena, *c.* 1948. The arena was opened in 1933. It was used for bathing beauty parades, talent contests, Easter bonnet and waistcoat parades, dance displays and so on. It certainly seems to have been a popular venue with the visitors (see below).

An enthralled audience at the Harbour Band Arena, *c.* 1950. The arena was open-air and could accommodate some 2,500 deckchairs. There is still an open-air stage in the area beside the Midland Hotel, but it is now surrounded by gardens.

Group of 'Miss Mildred's Olympic Girls', from Barrow, taking part in the Morecambe carnival parade of 1936. The carnival week in September was one of many initiatives to stretch the summer season. It evolved, largely, from the First World War peace celebrations in 1919. Crowds flocked to the carnival parades, and in 1936 there were an estimated 100,000 spectators.

Floats and crowds at the carnival parade, c. 1930. As well as the grand parade, the carnival week ended with an ox-roasting by the clock tower. In 1922 the public were charged 2d to baste the beast and 6d for a sandwich. The first slice was carved by the mayor and was offered in a sandwich to the Carnival Queen.

Crowning the Carnival Queen, Eva Withers of Manchester, in 1933. The mayor of Morecambe, William Gardner, is sitting to the left. The carnival stopped running in 1937 due to financial losses. However, it was revived in 1962 as a day event. It is now held in June and is still celebrated some thirty years later.

The illuminations going up in 1955. Morecambe claims to have been the first seaside town to install illuminations as an attraction. No date has been found to prove this claim. In 1924 a new power station on Caton Road boosted the town's electricity supply and allowed for full-scale, electric illuminations. That year some 40,000 coloured bulbs lit up the proms.

George Formby switching on the illuminations in 1950. During the Second World War – and indeed until 1949 – lighting restrictions had killed the illuminations. A well-known personality is invited to do the honours each year: Albert Modley the local comedian in 1960, Morecambe and Wise in 1969 (Eric Bartholomew taking his name from his home town), Eddie the Eagle in 1988, and Thora Hird and Helen Worth together (both Morecambe-born actors) in 1991.

The prom in 1955, originally captioned 'The Milky Way'. The earlier illuminations were simple strings of coloured lights. Later designs became more complicated, with themes or set tableaux.

Prizewinners of the 1932 Bonnie Baby Show, with the Carnival Queen and her attendants. This could be a very popular event. In 1935 there were some 500 hopefuls entered for the show, which was held at the Tower Ballroom.

Young performers in the Morecambe Music Festival practising on the prom, *c.* 1936. The competitive festival was held in the Winter Gardens and has always been of a high standard. A particular high point in its history was the presence of Sir Edward Elgar conducting one of his own pieces, 'Banner of St George', in 1905. The festival celebrated its centenary in 1990.

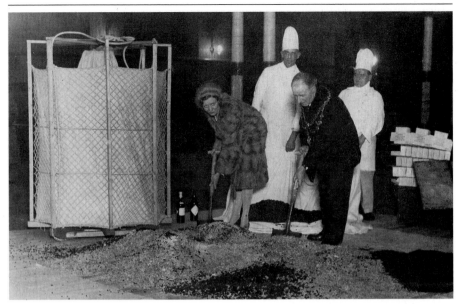

Councillor Fahy, mayor of Morecambe, mixing the giant Empire Christmas Pudding in the Winter Gardens in 1931. Following the recipe of the King's chef, Morecambe planned to cook the greatest pudding ever. It weighed 1,000 lb. Those interested in taking part could pay 2d a time to mix the pudding, using special spades. The mayor threw in ten half-sovereigns for good luck. Some 900 orders for portions arrived by post.

On 22 December a special gas boiler was lit by the clock tower. The pudding was boiled for sixty-eight hours. The great plan was not a success. Instead of the 8,000 anticipated servings the pudding had shrunk and only 4,500 portions were possible. Apparently it tasted awful. The takings did not cover the installation costs of the boiler and no one ever found the coins.

One of the heats in the first bathing beauty competition of 1945. Miss Great Britain started as a promotion for the Super Swimming Stadium. The competition was open to anyone between 16 and 26 years old and was run as a series of heats, on Wednesday afternoons, throughout June and July. The final was in August. Miss Great Britain for this year was Lydia Reid. She won seven guineas, a trophy and a basket of fruit.

Brenda Mee of Derby, winner of Miss Great Britain 1953. The *Sunday Dispatch* newspaper began sponsoring the competition in 1946. In 1957, on the demise of the *Dispatch*, Butlins took over sponsorship. Apart from prizes the winner often had 'official' engagements during her year as Miss Great Britain. Some began new careers too. Violet Pretty, winner in 1950, went on to a film career as Ann Heywood, and Debbie Greenwood (1984) became a television presenter.

Line up of the finalists in 1964. The competition faced criticism even in the early days. In 1946 the vicar of Morecambe commented: 'It seems a curious thing that a young woman can walk round before thousands of people as near naked as the law allows in order to have her physical points assessed as if she were some sort of prize animal at a cattle show.' In 1984 the competition was withdrawn from national television coverage. The last contest was in 1989 when Amanda Dyson of Barrow was the winner. In 1991 Pontins bought the title from the City Council and now hold the right to run the competition.

High seas on the front in the 1950s. Most of the photographs of Morecambe show fine-weather scenes. However, the resort has suffered damage – especially on the proms – from high tides and rough seas.

Storm damage in November 1977. The West End Pier was virtually destroyed in this storm. It was subsequently demolished, leaving Central Pier to stand alone. This second pier suffered two fires, one in 1987 and the other in 1991. It was finally removed in 1992.

Morecambe visitors really on holiday, busy doing nothing, *c.* 1950.

Fishing

Cocklers at Silverdale in the late nineteenth century. Cockling was a poorly-paid occupation often performed by large family groups, including young children. The Revd T. Rigg of Flookborough stated that 'Boys, girls, young men and women are out for hours together on the sands without the slightest control, and the results to morality might be imagined.'

A horse and cart, seen here at the turn of the century, were essential to transport cockles (and also mussels and fish) from the sands. Originally they were hawked around the district or sent from Hest Bank along the Lancaster Canal to market. From 1848 they were sent inland by train, which was very important in developing the Morecambe fishing industry.

Previous page: cocklers on the tidal sands of Morecambe Bay in the early twentieth century. Wooden boards with handles (jumbos) were used to pound the sand to bring the cockles to the surface. They were scooped into baskets (tiernels) using three-pronged forks (craams).

The two miles of rocky skears off the coast of Morecambe and Heysham have provided some of the most productive mussel beds in the country. At the turn of the century, when these photographs were taken, they were estimated to contain 90,000 tons of mussels at any one time. Here fishermen (above) are scraping mussels from the rocks using short-handled craams (rakes). The mussels were then collected in baskets in which they were also washed (below), before being heaped in the boats for the journey home. In Morecambe the industry employed over one hundred men full-time.

Once ashore the mussels were riddled (sorted), cleaned and bagged, seen taking place here on the promenade beside the Calton Landing Stage (pleasure boat) Company's hut at the top of Lord Street, Morecambe. This frequently took up to two hours at the end of a long period of gathering between tides.

Well-known musseller James Swain holding a long-handled craam. The heads of these fearsome-looking rakes were often 3 feet wide and the shaft up to 20 feet long. This enabled mussels on submerged skears to be gathered from a boat, using the net attached to the head of the craam. Traditionally, mussellers had paid the Lords of the Manor of Heysham for the right to exploit the fishery. The arrival of the railways increased demand and enhanced the value of the beds leading to increased fishing charges. The mussellers took the issue to court in 1874 and won their case. Subsequent evidence was unearthed, however, which undermined the justice of the award, but too late.

Tourists embarking for a trip on Morecambe Bay. The mussel season lasted from September to April so the mussel boats (foreground) were adapted for summer tourist use, many taking visitors for fishing trips before breakfast. It is said that because their wives ran the boarding houses, the excursion operators dared not be late back.

The Morecambe Bay fishing boat *Titbits*, built by Crossfield's, Arnside, for Harold Mount, Morecambe. This is one of the oldest photographs of the prawner type (also called the Lancashire nobby), seen on the foreshore at Morecambe probably shortly after her launch on 17 May 1893. Hundreds of these boats were built for local fishermen mainly involved in trawling for shrimps, which became the famous Morecambe delicacy. Although there were larger prawners, the most common size was 25 to 30 feet in length (stem to stern). They were well adapted to local sea conditions and designed for speed so that the catch could be brought ashore and marketed as quickly as possible. The boats were crewed by one or two men, often family members. Harold Mount's son, Jack, joined him fishing full-time at the age of 10 in 1892. One of Jack's earliest memories was being blown on to Pilling Marsh in a severe gale on 2 October 1895. He was carried to safety by his father and the following morning *Titbits* was pulled to Knott End by local farm horses and refloated. A number of other fishermen drowned.

Jack Mount, behind, and his assistant (who sold hot peas in local pubs and was inevitably nicknamed 'hot peas') preparing a catch aboard a prawner possibly during the 1940s. The shrimps were riddled (sieved) and boiled in salt water in what was sometimes called a 'tallegoram', a stove originally coal-fired. Here, only the chimney is visible.

Shrimps being riddled and bagged in a wooden tub (right) ready to be processed ashore. The trawl gear and net, towed along the sea bed attached to an 18-foot wide wooden beam, is here stowed on deck. The wooden bobbins attached to the net's ground rope are clearly visible.

Nearly all the Morecambe fishermen were self-employed and they relied heavily on the work of the family – especially in shrimping. As soon as the catch was landed it was taken home where the women and children were responsible for the arduous work of picking (shelling) and bagging the shrimps. They were either sold locally or to middlemen, who often exploited individual producers. To overcome this problem a number of fishermen established the Morecambe Trawlers Co-operative Society Ltd in 1919. It jointly processed and marketed the catch and successfully increased members' income. By June 1921 there were sixty-six members. Many women continued to process

the shrimps at home for the co-operative, but newly-built premises on Clarence Street enabled this to be done centrally also. Here, according to the *Visitor* newspaper in 1921, 'picking is carried on . . . under the best and cleanest conditions possible. This provides employment for about 30 girls, and the accompanying photograph [above] indicates the congenial conditions under which they work.' Nevertheless, behind them a sail has been hung to keep out draughts. Fourth from the right, at the head of the table, is Isabel Willacy who supervised the pickers.

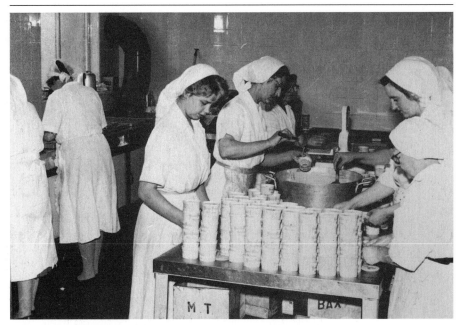

The Morecambe firm of James Baxter & Son is famous for its potted shrimps and in 1964 received a royal warrant to supply the Queen and Queen Mother. Here, 2-oz cartons are being filled by Margaret Willacy (fourth from left), Peggy Allan (front right) and Kathleen Willacy (behind).

Much of the day's catch was bagged up and taken from the promenade by handcart. Here, Tom and Ted Baxter (right) are at the top of Queen Street, Morecambe, probably heading for the fishermen's co-operative on Clarence Street, 1920s.

Morecambe carnival float belonging to the fishermen's co-operative outside their Clarence Street premises, 1925. They used real fish and won the £10 first prize. Left to right: Dick Threlfall, Robert Threlfall, Tom Hodgson, George Willacy, Harry Allan (in beard), Barton Baxter, Dick Baxter, William Baxter, David Willacy and (on the ground) Martin Allan and Percy Baxter.

Morecambe fisherman and fishmonger John Thomas Woodhouse holding a plate and molenger measure (quart size) used for measuring out shrimps. He was originally a mussel fisherman and later bought the fishing boat *Celeste* for shrimping during the summer months.

Many cockle fishermen also fixed stake nets on the sands. The nets were up to 300 yards long and attached to wooden stakes 3 feet high. During the ebb tide they funnelled fish into net bags such as the one held by this unknown fisherman in 1956.

Birds diving on a pool inside a fishing baulk (or 'bawk') on Morecambe foreshore, structures said to date from medieval times. At the turn of the century, when this photograph was taken, there were around fifteen of these fish traps in operation. On the ebb tide the tall oak and hazel walls of the 'V'-plan baulks funnelled the fish into a net 'box' at the apex of the trap, where they were collected at low tide.

Jack Aldren at J.T. Woodhouse's fishmongers in Morecambe's West End, possibly in the 1920s. Seals were rare in Morecambe Bay and this one was caught in a fishing baulk on the foreshore.

The Morecambe & Heysham Fishermen's Association was formed in 1893 and operated its own lifeboat. A new vessel, *Sir William Priestley*, was ordered from Fred Crossfield (right) and launched here at Arnside in 1934. The lifeboat is preserved today at the Lancaster Maritime Museum.

A Morecambe Bay prawner on a pleasure trip off Arnside before the First World War. The boatbuilders, Crossfield's of Arnside, were largely responsible for the development of the type from around 1850. In 1912 a 32-foot prawner cost around £60 and could be built in under four weeks.

A group of mussellers preparing their boats for public trips during the summer season before the vessels were inspected and licenced by the Corporation. The man standing with hands in pockets, left, is Jack Bell, and right foreground is 'Happy Jack' Woodhouse. They are on the site of the present-day Headway Hotel, Morecambe.

The Central Paddling Pool, Morecambe, was a favourite place for model yacht racing. Between the wars it was a hobby followed enthusiastically by the local fishermen, who founded the Morecambe Model Yacht Club. It held regular competitions and, according to one fisherman, 'there was hardly a model yachtsman among 'em hadn't a medal on his watch chain'. Left to right: J.T. Woodhouse (shrimper and pleasure boatman), Ted Hudson (musseller and cockler), the young Joe Thompson and, kneeling, Dick Woodhouse (shrimper).

James Rogerson of Morecambe shrimping with a hand (or push) net in the River Keer, near Carnforth, 1942. The net was pushed through the shallows, often for long periods. The catch was carried in a hamper slung on the fisherman's back.

Ownership of the Lune fishery has been highly prized since the Middle Ages and river bailiffs were employed to fend off poachers. Some bailiffs employed in the Beaumont fishery lived in these houses in Main Street, Skerton, which were demolished in the 1960s. The carved salmon wall stone is dated 1650 and is now displayed in the Lancaster Maritime Museum.

Fisherman William Townley at Sunderland Point, March 1932. His traditional-style tiernels (baskets) were used to collect and carry mussels, cockles and fish.

Unknown haaf- (or heave-) net fisherman at Bazil Point near Overton, 1890s. This method of catching salmon and sea trout has long been used on the Lune and other major rivers in the North West. A net fixed to an 18-foot wide wooden (or aluminium) beam on three legs is placed across the current (see below). When a fish swims into the net it is killed with a club known as a 'nep', or 'killer'. This form of fishing is still practised on the Lune and limited by National Rivers Authority licence to around twenty nets.

Haaf-netting on the Lune near Ashton Hall, 1934. At one time it was legal to form a powerful barrier across the current using a number of haaf-nets. Conservation needs now forbid the practice. The fishermen are, from left to right, William Alston, Richard Shaw, Jack Jackson and James Wilson.

A group of shipyard workers and fishermen examining a fine sturgeon at Glasson Dock. It was caught in the river at the turn of the century by James 'Shirley' Gardner, William Townley and G. Bagot of Sunderland Point. It was sent to London and sold for £5 5s.

Fishermen beside the Lune at Bazil Point relaxing outside one of their huts (seemingly built of driftwood) used to store fishing gear. This photograph shows their typical costume of moleskin trousers, waders, guernseys and a nice variety of headwear.

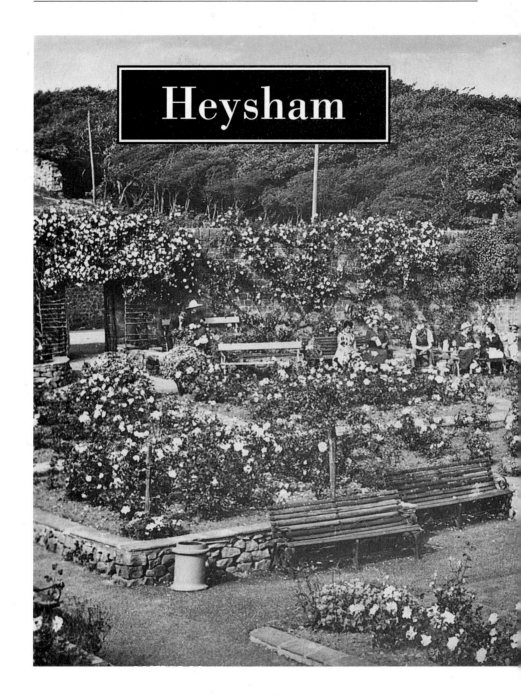

Heysham

The Old Hall in Higher Heysham was built by Robert Edmondson in 1598 and restored by the rector C.T. Royds in 1888. In 1914 the building was described as a farmhouse, 'standing back some distance from the road, from which it is separated by a well-kept garden and high fence wall'. Today the area has been swallowed up by housing, the building is a public house (the Old Hall Inn) and the garden is a car park. After St Peter's church and St Patrick's chapel, the Old Hall remains the oldest surviving building in Heysham.

Previous page: Heysham Head House was built in the reign of George III (1738–1820) on what is said to have been the site of the medieval manor. The Old English rose gardens were laid out by Septimus Wray, who, according to the official guidebook, was 'experienced in the layout of pleasure gardens in the Ilkley area'. Earlier this century the site incorporated a menagerie, including Teddy the Russian bear whose summer quarters were a caged and concreted enclosure. Here, according to the guidebook, he 'amused the visitors with his clever antics'. Heysham Head continued as a popular seaside attraction until the 1970s.

The lane leading down to the shore at Heysham village, which provided the main access to the sands for local fishermen. In 1825 Baines stated that ninety-three Heysham families were employed in agriculture (many in fishing also), nine in trade, handicraft and manufacture, and four in professional pursuits or unemployed. Visitors were reported to be 'more select than numerous'.

The ruined chapel on Heysham Head is of Saxon foundation and dedicated to St Patrick. He is said to have been shipwrecked nearby on his way from Ireland. The site was 'tidied up' by the rector John Royds in 1863–4, and in 1903 the ruin's foundations were strengthened. In the foreground is a group of remarkable rock-cut graves which date from the Dark Ages. They are thought to be unique in this country.

The Village.

The Dock

Heysham Church

The Shore

HEYSHAM
Nᴿ MORECAMBE

South Cottage

A postcard, *c.* 1910, recording prominent Heysham landmarks, including South (or Bay) Cottage on the shore north of the village. It was eventually demolished after storm damage and is now the site of a children's play area. Heysham was a popular excursion from nearby Morecambe, especially the picturesque old village and the ancient parish church of St Peter.

The 24th Lancashire Artillery Volunteers with four 32-pounder cannons near the old windmill, used as an arms and ammunition store. The figure in the centre with the sword is Captain Richard Coupland. Gunnery practice was obviously needed. In 1879 the Leeds Volunteer Artillery inadvertently struck the paddle steamer *Roses* sailing out in the bay. The offending cannon-ball can still be seen on display in Morecambe Town Hall.

Heysham Urban District Council succeeded the parish authorities in 1899. By the 1920s, however, there was a feeling that Heysham's interests would be better served through amalgamation with Morecambe, providing a sounder financial base and a local authority better able to provide the necessary services and develop the area's tourist potential. The Morecambe Corporation Act was passed in 1928 and the official ceremony took place on 1 October outside the Battery Hotel. The photograph shows the marriage ceremony underway on a platform raised over the old district boundary. Clasping hands (from left) are: H. Midgley, chairman of Heysham UDC, Alderman Travis Clegg JP and William H. Gardner JP, mayor of Morecambe and the new combined borough. Front right is Joseph Entwhistle, Morecambe town clerk. Others include Sir Alfred Bates (sixth from left), and behind the mayor, Alderman Banks. After the long speeches 2,000 free ice-cream cornets were distributed to the schoolchildren, while the grown-ups extended the celebrations with a banquet at the Morecambe Tower followed by dancing in the Balmoral Room.

Heysham's sleepy, old-world charm was rudely shattered in the 1890s when the Midland Railway began to construct a new cross-Channel ferry port. In 1896 the *Standard* newspaper stated that prior to this scheme 'the monkey which was once washed up at Middleton, just below Heysham, had provided the principal excitement in this haven of tranquil delights'. When it was completed in 1904 the port was claimed to be the most advanced in the world, operated entirely by electricity and designed for rapid and convenient rail access. This photograph, taken sometime around 1960, shows the harbour much as it was constructed. The Fish Quay (bottom left) was intended to encourage Morecambe and Fleetwood fishing boats to use the harbour, although this was never a great success. Further up, just below the North Quay, was the oil pontoon built for the Normandy landing in 1944 and installed at Heysham harbour by Shell in 1947. It was used for loading and bunkering ships and was towed away in 1977. Beyond the top of the harbour can be seen the remains of the reservoir, fed from an artesian well, which was built in 1904 to supply water to the whole site. Livestock sheds line the railway (top right) near the harbour power station which also supplied electricity to the local railway. On the South Quay is the impressive complex of goods sheds, and behind, the passenger railway station.

The harbour construction work was contracted to Messrs Price & Wills of Westminster in 1897. It was a mammoth undertaking covering a 350-acre site. Huge quarries and spoil tips were developed to build the two main breakwaters behind which was excavated the harbour basin. Altogether 1,115,148 cubic yards of spoil were removed, much by 'steam navvy' and horse-drawn, rail-mounted 'muck wagons' (above) and the use of pick and shovel (below). Explosives were also used extensively and caused a number of deaths and injuries. Labourer Henry Egerton, for example, lost both eyes during quarrying work, and in 1904 his compensation was fixed at half his wage, or 8s 11d per week. In 1901 Price & Wills were satisfied at their record of three to four fatalities, although the numbers maimed and injured must have been significant.

To cater for a resident labour force of 700 men a construction camp was built known as Klondyke. Nearby, an independently-operated camp also emerged and was named Dawson City. Klondyke contained, among other things, a bakery, grocery shop and hotel. The police station (far right) was sensibly placed next door to Blake's canteen, where much heavy drinking took place. There were a large number of houses for family occupation as well as male dormitories known either as 'fourpenny' or 'sixpenny' huts according to the weekly cost of lodging. The fourpenny huts were less comfortable and accommodated seventy-four. They were looked after by only two men, described as 'bedmaker and kitchen man'. The camps were built mostly of timber, tarpaulin and corrugated iron and were eventually demolished. All usable fittings from Klondyke were disposed of in a public sale in 1904.

This postcard view was taken shortly after the harbour was completed in 1904. The main development occurred here at the southern side of the 36-acre harbour basin. In addition to the goods sheds and station (off the picture, top left), there were a number of livestock sheds and paddocks for cattle, horses, pigs and geese brought from Ireland.

Much of the land round about was used for pasture, where livestock could recover after their voyage and before their onward rail journey to market. This advantage was stressed by the Midland Railway. Altogether, by the time the harbour opened, the project had cost over £3 million at 1900 prices.

The harbour station was spacious, had well-appointed waiting and refreshment rooms and even an overhead electric lift to transfer luggage to the waiting steamships. From July 1904 local railway services were provided by two steam railcars, or 'motor coaches' (left). In the first week of operation over 9,000 passengers arrived at the harbour, many of whom were sightseers who paid 3d for the twelve-minute trip from Morecambe. In 1908 the Heysham–Morecambe–Lancaster line was electrified and continued in use until 1966. The station was demolished in 1972, replaced by a new building in 1970 just before the collapse of the Irish traffic.

The harbour was designed for maximum cargo-handling efficiency. Goods were taken from steamships at the South Quay by rail-mounted cranes and elevators and loaded onto the railway wagons (left). The Dublin Shed, in this photograph of the 1920s, was used by Laird Line ships which provided a regular service between Heysham and Dublin until 1928.

The entrance to Heysham harbour was built near to the deep-water channel known as Heysham Lake. A new 900-foot long channel was cut to link them, but silting led to what became known as the 'Battle of the Sands' in which four dredgers were constantly employed to keep the channel open. The problem was eventually solved between 1909 and 1911 when the south jetty was built, creating a scour past the harbour entrance. Temporary railway lines on the jetty were used to tip stone and rubble alongside.

To coincide with the opening of Heysham harbour the Midland Railway ordered a fleet of four magnificent new steamships to ferry passengers and goods to and from Northern Ireland and the Isle of Man. One of these, the John Brown-built *Antrim*, became the first major steamer to dock at the newly-opened port, seen here shortly after her arrival on 31 May 1904. To mark the occasion the harbourmaster, Captain Myddleton Beasley, was ready on the South Quay to receive *Antrim*'s mooring ropes personally. The event was only slightly marred by a terrific sandstorm so that, according to the second engineer Percy Hughes, the area 'looked more like the Sahara Desert'.

Two vessels in the harbour between 14 and 18 September 1907 were the Bilbao-registered *Arechondo*, with iron ore for Carnforth ironworks, and the tiny schooner *Pool Fisher* – owned by James Fisher & Sons of Barrow-in-Furness – with wood for the Heysham bobbin mill. They are seen at the North Quay, which was specifically designed for the handling and storage of heavy goods, including pig iron, timber, slates and steel rails.

After the creation of the London Midland & Scottish Railway in 1923 Irish sailings were rationalized and Fleetwood's services transferred to Heysham. To cope with the extra traffic three new steamships, the *Duke of Lancaster, Duke of Rothesay* and the *Duke of Argyll*, were ordered from Denny's and delivered in 1928. The *Duke of Lancaster* was by far the unluckiest and between 1928 and 1939 she ran aground or collided with other vessels on at least six occasions. In her worst mishap she caught fire and sank at her moorings at the South Quay, Heysham harbour, in November 1931 (top). The following January she was salvaged (bottom) and returned to her builders for a refit lasting until June 1932.

During the 1950s Heysham's Irish traffic steadily increased. To replace the ageing *Dukes* of 1928 three new ships were ordered specifically for the transport of passengers, general cargo, mails, parcels and newspapers to and from Belfast. They were given the same names and entered service in 1956. To adapt to the new age of mass car ownership, both the *Duke of Lancaster* and the *Duke of Argyll*, seen here at Heysham, were converted into roll-on roll-off ferries in the late 1960s.

British Railways intended the ships to set 'a new high standard for passenger comfort' and they were aggressively marketed. The photographs here and on the facing page were taken on the *Duke of Argyll* by British Railways to illustrate the comfortable 'tasteful furnishings and spacious modern layout'. The 'passengers', however, are said to have been crew members posing for the camera.

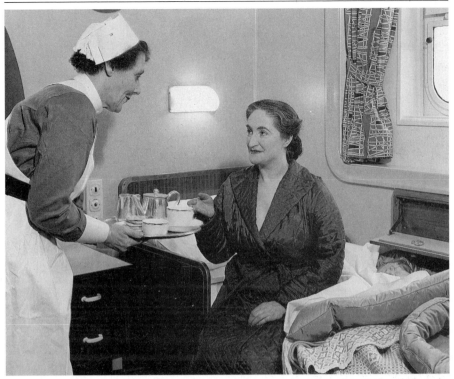

The ships were certainly well appointed, especially so in the first class accommodation. There were 240 first class cabins (above) and a further 216 in second class, although total passenger capacity was 1,800. Travellers in first class could enjoy the dining saloon (below), which seated seventy-six, while second class passengers made do with a combined lounge and café seating ninety-six. The Belfast service ended in 1975 and the *Duke of Argyll* was sold for educational cruising in the Mediterranean and renamed *Neptunia*.

The oil tanker *Linda Giovanna* discharging at the Ocean Oil jetty half a mile north of the entrance to Heysham harbour, 20–24 October 1967. This was the last occasion the jetty was used. Heysham's unlikely role as a major oil terminal was decided just before the Second World War. The Air Ministry needed high-octane fuel for its aircraft and a 250-acre site at nearby Middleton was chosen for the new Trimpell production complex. The 2,200-foot long concrete jetty was built to receive supplies of oil from the Caribbean and USA. It was fully commissioned in July 1941 and connected to the Trimpell site by underground pipeline. After the war the refinery was bought by Shell, who continued to operate much of the site. In 1967, however, an overland pipeline was built from Stanlow on the Mersey to supply oil to Middleton. The redundant Ocean Oil jetty was demolished in 1976 and the following year the refinery itself ceased production. Storage tanks and road tanker loading facilities continued in use until 1983.

Over the centuries many ships have come to grief in Morecambe Bay, including the barque *Vanadis* seen here at Half Moon Bay, Heysham. She was blown ashore on 22 February 1903 while on passage from Darien, Georgia, USA, to Fleetwood with a cargo of timber. Her crew were unharmed and eventually given breakfast by residents of Heysham village before their onward journey. The ship, from Mariehamn in Finland, was badly damaged and broken up on the spot, her cargo retrieved and taken away by horse and cart. A local blacksmith salvaged some of the yellow metal sheathing on the hull, which can still be found on the foreshore. In Nordic mythology 'Vanadis' is another name for the goddess of fertility, Freja, represented in the ship's figurehead. This, too, was retrieved and became a feature of the rose gardens at Heysham Head for many years.

Heysham Tower was built by T.J. Knowles around 1837 and was set in 13 acres of attractive gardens and wooded grounds. It was the home of the Cawthra family until the building of nearby Heysham harbour led them to move elsewhere. It was eventually taken over by the Midland Railway and opened as an hotel, charging 10s 6d for full board accommodation in 1907. In 1925 it became the Morecambe Bay Holiday Camp operated by Mr & Mrs B.S. Holden.

Heysham Tower accommodated a maximum 400 'campers' in the house and a further 100 (men only) in semi-permanent tents in the grounds. The 'holiday camp de luxe' was proud of its catering, serving four meals a day which were all included in the weekly cost of £2 5s in 1934.

The camp had a set of strict rules and regulations enforced by fines and, as a last resort, expulsion. Residents were kept occupied with PT, games, charabanc outings and steamboat trips. They appear to have had a jolly time. One diversion was the camp fire drill which, understandably, required the wearing of swimming costumes. They may also have discovered that their ladder was too short.

Lune Estuary

Sunderland Point photographer John Walker and river pilot James Spencer (with telescope), before 1898. Someone who knew him described Spencer as 'a short, stiff man with a face like the rising sun'. Sunderland was the base for Lune and Morecambe Bay pilots from at least the early 1700s.

Tugs were essential for towing sailing ships in and out of port and there was frequently cut-throat competition for towage work between the tugmasters. The Lancaster Port Commission operated a tug for this work, but here a rival – possibly the Fleetwood railway-owned tug *Fylde* (1881) – is towing a Norwegian barque downstream from Glasson Dock past Sunderland Point around 1900.

Previous page: Second Terrace, Sunderland Point, at the end of the nineteenth century. It was established as an outlying port for Lancaster in the early 1700s and remains remarkably unspoiled.

Wildfowlers beside their gun punt on the First Terrace, Sunderland Point, prospecting the Lune estuary. The gun is resting on trestles beside the canvas boat cover (left). Local residents supplemented their diet (and incomes) shooting lapwing, golden plover, curlew and duck. Traditionally some fishermen also used nets to catch dunlin, knots and oystercatchers out on the sands of Morecambe Bay (now strictly illegal).

The Lune estuary saw many ships founder. Here the Norwegian barque *Svalen* (1867) appears to have broken her back on the sands at Baithaven after being caught in a great gale on 4 June 1895. Her cargo of deals, for Lancaster timber merchant W. Huntingdon, was saved and the ship broken up on the foreshore some years later.

The jigger flat unloading timber onto horses and carts near the First Terrace, Sunderland Point. A temporary walkway has been built over the muddy foreshore. The vessel is probably the 70-ton *John & William* owned at Llandulas seen here in the late 1890s. She is also known to have delivered roadstone and tarmacadam.

The male population of Sunderland Point was employed almost entirely in fishing and pilotage in the Lune estuary and Morecambe Bay. In this photograph of the 1890s are (from left to right): Tom Spencer (1857–1935), pilot; young Gerard Bagot and Tom Gardner (1886–1952), both later pilots; Richard Bagot (1853–1927), pilot; Arthur Townley (1856–1933), standing at back, with daughter Jessie; Luke Gardner (1831–98); and James 'Shirley' Gardner (1869–1937), pilot for forty-seven years between 1890 and 1937.

Woodhouse's boatyard on Main Street, Overton, was well known for the quality of small craft it built for the local fishing and holiday industries. Sometimes, as in this photograph, it constructed yachts for wealthy local residents, although the details of this vessel are unknown. The last yacht built before the yard closed (after the First World War) was the *Sue*, reportedly still afloat on the River Fowey, Cornwall, in 1988.

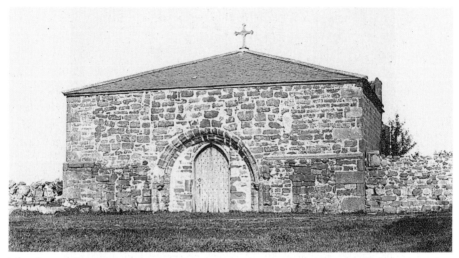

The thirteenth-century Chapter House at Cockersands, south of the Lune, is all that remains of the abbey built by Premonstratensian canons from Croxton Abbey, Leicestershire. In 1543, after the suppression, it was sold by the Crown to William Kitchen of Hatfield. His daughter, Ann, married Robert Dalton of nearby Thurnham Hall and the Chapter House was actively used as the Dalton family burial vault from the mid-eighteenth century until 1861.

The Upper Lighthouse of Cockersands was one of two built in the vicinity by the Port Commission in 1847 to guide ships entering the Lune. The 54-foot high wooden tower was designed by John B. Hartley, son of the famous Liverpool dock engineer Jesse Hartley, and cost £650. It was demolished in 1954, replaced by a functional, but characterless, steel tower with automatic electric lights. Photograph taken by George Gilchrist of Sunderland Point at the turn of the century.

Both lighthouses at Cockersands were tended by members of the Raby family from 1847 until December 1945. Janet Raby, seen here on 29 June 1943, was the last of the line. She is equipped for catching flounders (or flukes) in the shallows and channels at the edge of the river. The keepers exploited the local fishing to supplement their income. In 1946 Thomas Parkinson became keeper of the lighthouses for £2 per week and rent-free accommodation. When he was out fishing his wife Beatrice and son Robert attended to the arduous twice-daily regime of cleaning and maintenance.

The captain and crew of the three-masted schooner *Mary B Mitchell*. The ship came into Glasson Dock many times, although the precise date and location of this view is unknown. She was built in 1892 by P. Rodgers & Company, Carrickfergus, and was registered in Beaumaris, Anglesey, frequently carrying slates out of Penrhyn. Glasson Dock became a busy port during the mid-nineteenth century following the earlier

decline in eighteenth-century overseas trade with the West Indies and Baltic. The dock was opened in 1787 as, effectively, the new Port of Lancaster. It handled an increasingly wide range and quantity of industrial goods and building materials, utilizing the Lancaster Canal for distribution as far as Kendal and Preston.

Most of the ships visiting Glasson Dock in the late nineteenth century were involved in trade around the British coast or to the near continent. In 1890, 289 ships of all types, ranging in size from 23 to 798 tons, visited the port. Two typical examples were the schooner *Mary Waters* (1875), in the foreground, built and registered at Padstow, Cornwall; and the 124-foot long barque *Panama* (1869) built at Brake an der Weser, Germany, and registered at Pernau, Russia.

The Watch House at the entrance to Glasson Dock was built by the Lancaster Port Commission in 1836 for £19 3s. The tower appears to be in use as a greenhouse, possibly for growing tomatoes. To the left of the signal mast someone is posing on an arm of the capstan, used to open the dock gates. A chalked message on the London & North Western Railway wagon, right, suggests it is awaiting repair.

Regattas, involving boat races and sports, were universally popular before the First World War. The regatta at Sunderland Point was established as early as 1824, although all the early Luneside regattas were associated with disorder and drunkenness. They were revived at the end of the century, administered by 'respectable' local residents, as healthy and enjoyable family entertainment. Here swimmers are about to dive from a pontoon in Glasson Dock, 1912.

A Glasson shipyard dry dock Account Book records that 'On October 1 [1890] Graving Dock gates were carried away by a storm wave in a westerly hurricane. Barque *Alice* washed out and sunk.' The Norwegian vessel, seen here resting on the bottom of the dock, was involved in Glasson Dock's extensive timber trade with Canada and Scandinavia. Piles of timber, much of it used in the local construction industry, can be seen stacked on the East Quay, beyond, awaiting transportation by the London & North Western Railway Company.

The Lune estuary provided a convenient base for a number of wealthy local yachtsmen. It was a popular Victorian pastime and drew on the skills and experience of local fishermen, hired as crew, such as Tom Gardner of Sunderland Point who skippered Arthur Mansergh's yacht *Sue* (p. 133). Here the crew of the *Marinetta* and her owner, William Hatch and his wife, pose for their photograph in Glasson Dock. Although not sumptuously appointed, the interior (below) was comfortable enough for day cruises and trips along the coast.

William Hatch, a Lancaster timber merchant and contractor, kept the 63-foot long *Marinetta* at Glasson Dock. She was built in 1870 by A. Payne & Sons, Southampton, and appears to have been skippered locally by Wilfred Woodhouse. She was maintained by the Glasson shipyard and entered the dry dock (as here) on a number of occasions, firstly in 1898 soon after she was bought from Captain Willson of Sleaford, Lincolnshire. The vessel was sold to William Dobie of Dollar, Clackmannanshire, around 1909.

The *Success* masqueraded as 'the last of England's infamous felon fleet' which had transported thousands of convicts to Australia. In this guise she toured the coast as a 'floating museum' and arrived at Glasson Dock in October 1911. For 6d visitors were able to view the ship and its gruesome array of prisoner punishments. Before heading off to New York the *Success* was taken into Glasson dry dock for maintenance work. This overran by two weeks, causing the owner, Mr D.M. Smith, to cancel his passage on the *Titanic* which left Southampton on 10 April 1912.

The shipyard at Glasson was established in 1837 and depended on ship maintenance and repair work, rather than new building, for its success. The Brussels-registered barque *La Ville d'Ostend* arrived for repair in October 1885 and is seen here from the East Quay, dressed overall and presumably ready to depart.

Views of shipbuilding activities at Glasson are very rare. Here, in a detail of the previous picture, the workmen of Nicholson & Marsh can be seen lining the deck of a partially-completed schooner, possibly the *Ryelands* which was launched in 1887. This ship is better known as the *Moby Dick*, used in a number of Walt Disney films including *Moby Dick* and *Treasure Island*. She was later moored off Morecambe promenade as a tourist attraction before being destroyed by fire in 1970.

The wet dock at Glasson was designed by the Liverpool engineer Henry Berry and remains essentially the same today. The wooden dock gates, however, have been replaced a number of times, on this occasion probably during the winter of 1923–4. The work was done by Glasson ship repairers, Nicholson & Sons, for £4,700. New, wider steel gates were installed in 1987.

Unidentified steamships at Glasson Dock in the 1890s. At this time the harbour was becoming congested with vessels unloading cargoes of iron ore destined for Barton's ironworks at Carnforth. Other cargoes included china clay, linseed oil and Portuguese cork for the large oilcloth and linoleum factories at Lancaster, as well as feedstuffs for the livestock farms of North Lancashire and Westmorland.

Ships ceased being built by Nicholson & Sons at Glasson in 1907. Thereafter they concentrated on ship repair and re-tooled the yard to cater for the increasing number of steamships visiting the Lune. This unidentified vessel has been shored up with stout timbers ready for the water to be drained from the dock.

St George's Quay, Lancaster, seen here in the late 1800s, is a remarkable surviving port complex dating largely from the late eighteenth century. It was laid out and constructed from 1750 to cope with the town's prosperous West Indies and Baltic trade. The Port Commission built the quay wall from 1750 and sold off the land behind for warehousing and commercial use. A fine porticoed Custom House was also built in 1764 (extreme right), now occupied by the Lancaster Maritime Museum. This prosperous foreign trade declined after 1800 and the quayside was given over to the storage of less valuable goods including grain, often prepared as animal feed. Pye's warehouse (in front of the gasworks chimney) was used for this purpose until recent times. The quayside continued to be used for coastal trade throughout the nineteenth century. Business declined further, however, when larger ships were prevented from reaching St George's Quay because of the construction of the Lancaster–Carlisle railway bridge downstream in 1845. Due to the lack of trade the quay was transferred to the ownership of Lancaster Corporation in 1901. The quayside had a thriving community and the area included a number of public houses, shops, workshops and even (in 1866) a small dairy on Lune Street accommodating twelve cows. In 1881 the resident population of St George's Quay was 180, with a further 280 on the streets behind. Many lived in rented homes and worked at Lune Mills, Williamson's linoleum factory downstream. Many houses were condemned in the 1930s and subsequent demolitions behind the quayside have sadly destroyed much of the historic fabric. Happily most of the derelict warehouses have been converted into residential flats.

A fine view of the clipper *Wennington*, newly-launched and fitting out at New Quay, Lancaster, 1865. The ship was ordered by the original Liverpool White Star line, established in 1845 by the Lancaster-born shipbroker Henry Threlfall Wilson and partner John Pilkington. They concentrated on the prosperous emigrant trade to Australia, for which fast passages were required, and invested heavily in new clippers to outclass their rivals. Wilson had originally proposed that the commercial community of Lancaster establish the Lune Shipbuilding Company to profit from the demand for iron clippers. The yard was created in 1863 and *Wennington* was the first ship to be built. The launching ceremony was performed by Mrs Saunders of Wennington Hall, wife of

the company chairman. The event captured the popular imagination and 15,000 people were said to have lined the river banks. The White Star line went bankrupt in 1867 and the partners were left owing £527,000. The *Wennington* was sold to the Lancaster Ship Owners Company, with whom Wilson found another job as manager. The ship was lost in the Java Sea in 1878. The White Star name and goodwill was sold to Thomas Henry Ismay to become the famous transatlantic line of later years. The Lune Shipbuilding Company lasted until 1870, having built fourteen vessels of different types and size. The firm suffered the effects of intense shipbuilding competition, an unsuitable site and poor management.

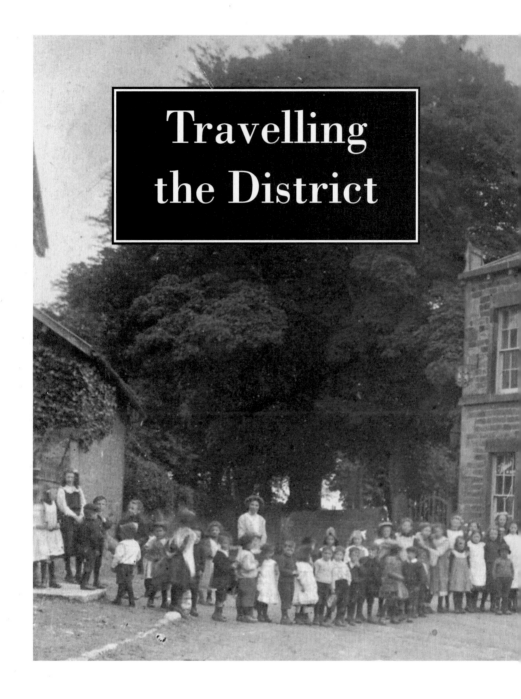

Travelling
the District

Main Street in Skerton, *c.* 1890. Skerton was a separate village from Lancaster, just north of the River Lune, until boundary changes were made in 1886. Many of its residents worked across the river, especially in the great linoleum works of James Williamson whose town-house 'Ryelands' is also in Skerton.

Flats in Main Way, Skerton, *c.* 1960. By the 1950s much of Skerton's terraced housing was in poor repair and, in line with planning views at the time, was scheduled for major redevelopment. In the case of Main Way this comprised clearing Main Street (above) and the Ramparts, straightening the old road line and building a series of high-rise flats.

Previous page: group of young children outside the Blue Anchor Hotel, Bolton-le-Sands, 1908. Perhaps this group are on a Sunday school outing. This pretty village was one that was often visited on outings.

Pleasure boating on the Lune in front of Halton Hall, from a postcard postmarked 1907. Originally Halton was a major manor consisting of twenty-two townships in the area. It boasted a small-scale coated-fabric business in the mill by the river. Halton Water is deep, still and wide and so has always been popular for boating. It is still used by the grammar school, university and John o'Gaunt rowing clubs. In the great freeze of 1892–3 you could skate on the Lune all the way from Skerton Bridge to Halton.

Hest Bank fête, c. 1906. The occasion for the fête is unknown. Perhaps it was the one noted in the local paper as a fund-raising venture for the new Hest Bank Golf Club – formed in 1905 and admitting 'ladies' from the outset.

Afternoon tea in the garden of the Hest Bank Hotel, from a coloured postcard postmarked 1907. The hotel (or inn as it was then) was the starting point for the dangerous route across Morecambe Bay. Before the opening of the railway, over-sands coaches left daily for the journey. It is said that the hotel was used to guide travellers across the sands by placing a huge lantern in the large window to the right.

Postcard view along Coastal Road, with Morecambe Bay in the background, postmarked 1905. From the early 1800s the village tried to attract people for the new, fashionable idea of seabathing. As early as 1815 the Hest Bank Inn boasted a new bathing machine 'for the better accommodation of sea-bathers'. In 1857 the arrival of the railway made people far more mobile and Hest Bank became a fashionable place to visit. Just visible in the background is the station, with its footbridge over the railway line.

The canal at Hest Bank, drained after subsidence during drainage excavations, March 1895. Luckily the disaster happened overnight so no one was hurt. However, the railway line – running alongside the canal – was strewn with debris and was temporarily closed, and Station Road lost all its tarmac and gravel in the flooding. Many local people made their way up to view the scene on the first Wednesday (half-day) after the event. The local paper reported several amateur photographers taking snapshops of the scene. Perhaps this is one.

Bank House, on the canal at Bolton-le-Sands, c. 1905. The canal from Preston, via Lancaster, passed through Bolton-le-Sands to Tewitfield in the first phase of construction, 1797. This brought both goods and passengers. The handsome house seems to date from the early 1800s. The village, nestling between the canal and the railway, was noted as a summer resort for those wanting a quiet holiday near the coast.

The Catholic church, St Mary of the Angels, Bolton-le-Sands, *c.* 1905. In 1868 a temporary place of worship was established in a barn and was used until this fine church was consecrated in 1884. Note the charabanc party outside the Blue Anchor Hotel, with several willing children trying to sell produce from their baskets to the visitors. The original building of the Blue Anchor was erected in 1706.

Postcard of Market Street, Carnforth, postmarked 1914. The town stood at the junction of the Furness and Midland Railway and the London and North Western Railway. The station was built in 1880, for joint use of the different railway companies, and was immortalized in the cinema classic *Brief Encounter*, released in 1945 and starring Celia Johnson and Trevor Howard. A flavour of the town's railway heritage is still available in the old engine sheds at Steamtown.

The Zeppelin *Hindenberg*, photographed over the back of Hewthwaite Terrace, Carnforth, 22 May 1936. The Zeppelin was also captured on film, over Quernmore, where the Nazi swastika is clearly visible.

Postcard view of Washington House, Warton, postmarked 1916. Ancestors of George Washington – the first President of the USA – hailed from Warton. Robert Washington built the church of St Oswald here in the fifteenth century. The last of the family to live in the village was Thomas Washington, vicar of Warton from 1799 to 1823, who is buried in the churchyard. The link with America is maintained when, every 4 July, the Stars and Stripes flag is flown on the church tower.

Borwick Hall with its farm buildings, c. 1900. The hall was built around 1590 by Robert Bindloss, incorporating an earlier pele tower. Much of it was refurbished in the 1930s. This is probably around the time William Woodhouse, a local artist, painted a number of romanticized interiors of the hall. Many incorporated figures of cavaliers. During the civil war, however, the Bindloss family sided first with Parliament and then became Royalists some time before the Restoration. The building is now owned by Lancashire Youth Clubs Association, providing accommodation and training facilities.

Town End, Caton, with the village children gathered on the 'Fish-Stones', c. 1885. The local story is that monks from Cockersand Abbey brought their Lune salmon here for sale. Today the massive oak tree has a preservation order on it. Caton was not a purely agricultural village – it boasted one of Storey Bros. cotton mills (Low Mill) which is currently being refurbished as housing. Caton's Victoria Institute celebrated its centenary in 1988.

Main Street, Hornby, c. 1905. The gentleman in the gateway to the right is standing in front of the schoolroom grounds. This was built in 1875 and was used until the new school over the bridge opened in the 1960s. The bridge over the River Wenning was built in 1769 and was widened during the Second World War. Presumably this was also the time the schoolroom railings disappeared. Hornby Castle is largely nineteenth century in its construction, although it stands on the site of a Norman foundation and possibly a Roman villa.

Conder Green hamlet, with the Stork public house, *c.* 1905. The hamlet came under the township of Ashton-with-Stodday. This was an agricultural area with wheat, oats, potatoes and clover as the main crops. The scene has changed little, but the road from Lancaster to Cockerham and Glasson Dock is now quite busy.

Ashton Hall, *c.* 1905, from a postcard by Davis & Sons. At this date the Hall belonged to James Williamson, the linoleum magnate. On gaining his peerage in 1895, he took his title from this property – becoming Baron Ashton of Ashton. He had bought the Hall in 1884 from the widow of Colonel Starkie. They, in turn, had purchased the property from the Duke of Hamilton and had virtually rebuilt it. Lord Ashton used it as a country residence and had a small golf course in the grounds. Since 1933, appropriately, it has been the home of Lancaster Golf Club.

Thurnham Roman Catholic School on Moss Lane, *c.* 1905. This area had a strong Catholic tradition. The local landowners, the Daltons of Thurnham Hall, were of the faith and in 1780 had supported the first local Catholic chapel with a grant of land for building. In John Dalton's will of 1837 money was left for a new church and for the school. The bungalow on the right was the original schoolroom and may date from this time. The schoolhouse was next door. The newer building to the left was added in the 1880s, when the original was deemed too small. In 1953, with fewer children in the area, the school was closed and the remaining pupils were moved to surrounding schools. The buildings are now converted to housing.

Galgate silk mill, *c.* 1900. This was a water-powered corn mill, established in 1792, that was converted to silk spinning. The larger mill buildings were added in the 1840s. The firm closed down in 1971 and the buildings are now used as shop units and showrooms. This thriving village was the first in the area to install a branch of the Lancaster Co-op, in May 1861, just four months after the main shop opened. The sign of the beehive, the Co-op's logo, is still visible on the building on the main road.

A traveller in the district, with his accordion and monkey, photographed by John Walker, *c.* 1900. This travelling player may have belonged to one of the gypsy communities that visited the area regularly. In 1902 an unfortunate incident was reported in the press. Army volunteers had come to blows with gypsies camping in the woods by Hest Bank station. As a result the gypsies were cleared from the area to travel once again.